Agile Product Management:

Product Owner

27 Tips To Manage Your Product And Work With Scrum Teams

Introduction

Thank you and congratulations on taking this class, *"Product Owner: 27 Tips To Manage Your Product And Work With Scrum Teams"*.

In this class, you will be given a multitude of proven tips to effectively create a product and work with scrum teams.

I am confident that this class will enable you to learn a multitude of skills since it starts by giving you a full introduction to the concept of scrum and agile product development, scrum and agile principles and a host of other valuable information that will give you a full understanding of the topic. I then walk you through the process of understanding your role as a product owner, how your role differs from that of a traditional product manager, how to create products and a lot more. Once you've learnt all that, I will then give you valuable tips for effectively creating a product and working with teams. As you go through the class, you will come across a wide range of practical examples that you can use to understand the scrum framework a lot better. To break this class into easy to digest parts, you will learn:

- A brief recap of agile and scrum, its principles and other concepts involved in scrum

- What your job as a product owner entails and how your work differs from that of a typical product manager

- How to create a product using the scrum framework

- How product creation in scrum differs from other agile frameworks like the Waterfall method.

- How to create a product roadmap

- 27 tips that you can follow to create your product and to manage your scrum team

So let's get started and let me teach you how to improve product backlog management.

Table of Contents

Before we learn about the helpful tips that you can follow to work with teams while developing a product, let's start by building a good understanding of what scrum is all about.

Scrum Methodology: The Basics

What Is Agile?

Agile is an umbrella term for a set of values, principles, methods and frameworks, all of which adhere to the agile manefesto. Many of the agile methods entail building products incrementally right from the onset as opposed to delivering the completed software in one project. The idea is to deliver projects that align to company goals and customer needs in pieces, very fast. So in essence, this approach encourages regular inspection as well as adaptation along with accountability, teamwork and self organization. For this to work, a project has to be broken down into tiny user functionality bits that are usually described as *user stories*, which are then prioritized after which they are delivered within short cycles referred to as *iterations* (often 21 to 4 weeks). The concept of agile was developed to provide an alternative software development methodology to counteract the snags intraditional sequential development. The power of agile lies in its ability to allow teams to respond to unpredictability through increasable, repeatable work stages.

What Is Scrum?

As discussed, there are several types of software development methodologies falling under the umbrella term 'agile' of which scrum is one. The name scrum was inspired by the rugby scrums and the way they work together in the team with the same objective. Scrum is a framework, which has been in use in the management of complex product development. It is not really a process or a technique for building products. Instead, scrum is a framework that you can use to employ different techniques and processes. In essence, scrum helps to make clear the relative efficacy of your product development and management practices to enable you to improve. The framework is made up of scrum teams along with their associated roles, events (meetings), artifacts as well as rules. For scrum to work well, each component within a framework usually serves a certain purpose. Its rules usually bind together a set of events, roles as well as artifacts that usually govern the relationships and interactions between them.

Scrum is the most popular and the most outstanding of the different frameworks for implementing agile especially due to its concepts (which are very specific), and the practices, which are categorized into time boxes, roles and artifacts. And although you can still use scrum for other projects, it is mainly used in software development since these projects often have requirements that change very fast. Scrum follows the same principles as agile, to ensure that the processes of product development are handled in a more efficient way than the traditional development processes, but it also has its own principles different from the other agile frameworks in the same way they differ among each other.

Scrum is based on empirical process control theory, a theory, which consists of 3 basic pillars that we've already mentioned earlier: transparency, inspection and finally adaptation. Empiricism in this case asserts that knowledge usually comes from experience and making various decisions on what is actually known. Scrum uses an iterative, incremental approach in order to optimize predictability as well as control risk. Through utilization of the three pillars, no one in the production team can withhold information from the group. All the info is displayed for every stakeholder to know exactly what is going on at each level and in each sprint. Transparency (honesty) is practiced by having every member of the team to have his/her say before any new product functionality is completed with the goal of creating trust between team members. So in essence, product functionality is not done until the team says it is done. As for inspection, the team has to be ready to thoroughly look into a product's features (through reviews) and team's processes (through retrospectives) and if need be, employ adaptation by changing any part that is not satisfactory to the product owner, team members and to the other stakeholders who can add their input or question the work being done on the product at any time.

Scrum is as a 'time boxed' software development framework. So what does this 'time boxed' mean? Let's take a closer look at what this means.

The Time-Boxed Element Of Scrum

Time boxing is used as a planning technique where each schedule is divided into a number of separate time periods called sprints. Each sprint has its own deliverables, deadline, and sometimes a budget. Besides this, even short activities are time-boxed e.g. all meetings are time-boxed to ensure efficient use of available time i.e. Daily Scrum Meetings, Sprint Planning Meetings, Sprint Retrospective Meetings and Sprint Review Meetings.

Generally, **scrum framework is made up of several components namely**:

Sprints

At the heart of scrum is a sprint, which essentially refers to a time box of a month or less within which the team creates a potentially releasable, 'done' or useable increment of a product. Sprints have consistent durations throughout a certain development effort. Moreover, a new sprint usually starts immediately a previous sprint is concluded.

A sprint usually contains and consists the different sprint events/meetings (as discussed below). During each sprint:

✓ There are no new changes made that may endanger the sprint goal

✓ The quality of all goals does not decrease

✓ The scope of work may be re-negotiated or clarified between the product owner and the development team as they learn more.

Note: A sprint takes no more than 1 month. And like normal projects, sprints are usually used to accomplish a certain goal. So in essence, each sprint will have a definition of what to build, a design along with a flexible plan that guides you in building it, the work involved and the resultant effect/product.

Scrum Team (Also Referred To As The 3 Roles In Scrum)

The 3 roles involved in scrum include the product owner, the scrum master and the development team. We will discuss more on this briefly.

The scrum team

This team has three components; the product owner, the scrum master and the development team.

✓ The product owner

This is the person fully accountable for the successful delivery of a product in line with the business' goals. Although the product owner is in charge of the product, he/ she is, unlike in the traditional scenario, more of a collaborator than a commander and controller. As the bulk of this class is dedicated to the product owner, I will cover much more about this later.

✓ The scrum master

Is in charge of facilitating a self-organized development team, which embraces the same principles as in scrum which are transparency, inspect and adapt. He/she can be called scrum expert, adviser, or coach and is the guru in scrum matters.

Moreover, he or she works as a facilitator would in group learning. He/she should help both the development team and the product owner to understand the scrum way and live the scrum way. Since there are likely to be impediments along the way, the scrum master should find ways to remove or go over them. Nonetheless, although the scrum master is more knowledgeable about scrum than the product owner (in most cases), s/he is not the one in charge of decisions about products as that is the product owner's turf.

✓ *The development team*

The development team is cross-functional and comprises professionals like developers, testers, wordsmiths, builders (dependent on the domain.) However, although they have their own specializations, by the end of the development process, each should have learnt a little of the other. They are the people in charge of building the product, which can be a website, software, a building, a car etc. They should be empowered enough to self-organize themselves into delivering.

For the team to work effectively, it is essential that everyone in the team follows a common goal, adheres to the same guidelines, norms and rules and that they show each other respect. The decision about how the work is done rests upon them and none of them should think of a part of the process as 'not my job'. They are as autonomous as possible and although learning is required and expected, each team member should be working from his/ her comfort zone. They have to be self-organized and they have to work out ways to overcome impediments.

✓ *The product team's goal*

The team's goal is to harmoniously and respectfully work together to deliver a functional product within the time and budget confinements. If more than estimated is used, it should not be too much.

To achieve this, the Agile and Scrum forerunners put in place principles, which have to be implemented for the successful implementation of the process. These principles are written in stone and any individual or company who aims to use scrum should abide by them. There are specific roles for specific people in the implementation process.

Scrum Ceremonies

These essentially refer to all formal meetings and time-periods that are involved in scrum. They include sprint planning meetings, daily scrum, sprint review meetings and finally sprint retrospective meetings.

Sprint Planning Meetings: This is the first meeting the scrum team holds. In this meeting, the product owner makes clear the vision of the product, and the development team selects the features to work on from the product backlog. They decide how they will build the features, and estimate the duration required to complete the features.

Sprint Retrospective Meetings: In this meeting, the team members go through what transpired during the sprint to find out what they did right or wrong, they also consider the areas of improvement, things they can continue doing in future sprints, those they can start doing, and those they can stop.

Sprint Review Meetings: A sprint review meeting ensures the standards of product development to remain high. Stakeholders are invited to the meeting to review an increment of the product and give feedback to the team in order to improve it or move it in the right direction.

Daily Stand-up Meetings: In a daily stand-up meeting, the team looks back to the previous day's work and bring each other up to date on the work each team managed to do, what they intend to do, and any blockers they have to completing their work.

Scrum Artifacts

Scrum is made up of several artifacts namely:

✓ *Product increments*: As I already mentioned, at the end of every sprint, the resultant product increment ought to be in a functional state, which meets the scrum team's definition of 'done'. As such, if everything works perfectly well, the team's estimation is fairly perfect, the increment has all its sprint backlog's items tested and then documented.

✓ *Product backlog*: This refers to an ordered list of all the features that are needed as part of the end product. Moreover, it is the single source of all the requirements for any new changes that need to be made to a product. This refers to a prioritized backlog that features end user requirements, which is the product owner's property. The product backlog will often have features, enhancements, functions, fixes, and requirements that usually constitute changes that need to be made to the particular product in any future releases. In essence, the product backlog items often have the attributes of order, description, value and estimate. All these are termed as user stories. The person in charge of the product backlog is the product owner; he/she is responsible for its availability, content and ordering.

A sample of a sports website product backlog of estimated Stories Usually these are written on the front and back of user story cards (5 by 3 index cards) The images are usually stored elsewhere. Due to the large nature of the backlog, I have placed it on my blog with explanations. Just go to:

http://pashunconsulting.co.uk/blog/productbacklog.html *thats*
http://pashunconsulting.co.uk/blog/productbacklog.html

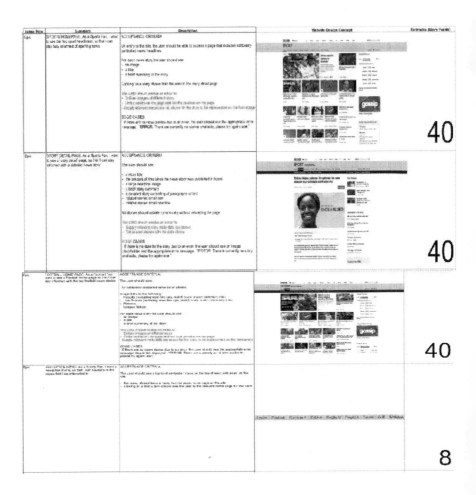

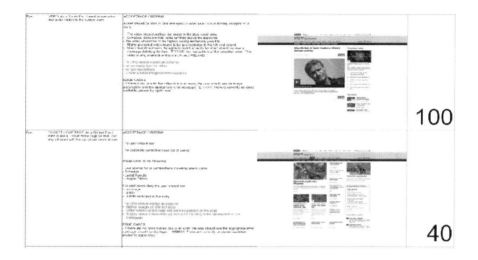

✓ *Sprint backlog*: This refers to a set of product backlog items that are selected for the sprint along with a plan for delivering the end product increment and then realizing the sprint goal. It is created during the sprint planning meeting. It is a forecast by the team with respect to what functionality will end up being made available in the next increment and the work that's needed in order to deliver the functionality as a working product increment. You can think of the sprint backlog as a plan that has enough detail, which the team can understand in order to track in the daily scrum. Normally, the team usually modifies the sprint backlog throughout the sprint and then the sprint backlog usually emerges during the sprint.

✓ *Sprint burn-down chart*: At any particular time in a sprint, it is possible to sum the total work that's remaining in the sprint backlog. The scrum team usually tracks the total work that's remaining for each daily scrum in order to project the probability of attaining the sprint goal. It is through close tracking that the scrum team can actually be able to manage its entire progress. A sprint burn down chart refers to the practice of trending the work that the scrum team expends. Using this has been proven to be an effective way of monitoring the progress of the sprint towards the attainment of the sprint goal. It is the responsibility of the product owner to track the work that's remaining at every sprint review. When the product owner compares the work remaining during reviews for previous sprints, he or she can then assess progress towards the completing the projected work by the desired time for that particular goal. All the information is then shared to stakeholders.

By now, you definitely have a basic idea of what scrum is all about. To help enhance your knowledge about scrum, let's discuss the different principles of scrum and agile.

Principles to remember

The following are some of the principles you can use to make projects successful

1. Active user participation is important and non-negotiable

Product end-users are stakeholders during the product development process and the scrum framework stipulates that they must actively participate in giving feedback to the product team for the betterment of the final product.

2. The development team must be nurtured to be decision makers

This is especially important because most of the time, each team member will be working each on his or her own. The product owner and the scrum master have to empower the development team so that they can make decisions freely when the need arises.

3. Obligations and conditions change but the sprint timescale remains consistent

As the process develops, there are things, which might change if need be in relation to the adaptability in the agile principles e.g. responsibilities and other conditions. However, the sprint is time is boxed meaning it is fixed and and increment of the product must be presented at the end of that time.

4. Requirements must be captured at a high level, which is both lightweight and visual

This means that when requirements to be followed are written down, there are various methods such as user stories, high level vision statements and storyboards that can paint the picture without needing to go into detail in early stages. The detail comes later with the help of the team.

5. There must be development of small releases, which are augmentable and can be redone

This means that individual iterations or sprints will lead to the complete product. The team should be flexible from sprint to sprint in order to respond to change. The culmination of each piece of the product is added together to make the finished product.

6. **Focus must be placed on regular delivery of products** and this is where the sprints come in to ensure releases are developed in each sprint. You should aim to release to the live environment as often as possible/necessary.

7. **Completion of each feature before moving on to the next is paramount** and if the feature is unfinished, it is moved back to the backlog as if it was never attempted. The team should avoid the situation where many features are partially done.

8. **Apply the 80/20 rule**; the rule is also known as the Pareto principle and it based on the belief that maximum benefits must come from very little work e.g. 20% effort producing 80% results. Therefore prioritizing the backlog is extremely important to ensure that the earliest work done is achieving most of the business goals.

9. **Testing must be incorporated throughout the project development process.**

There must be early and regular testing implemented to ensure that the team does not keep developing a product that is faulty yet they could have discovered . the issue had they tested early.

10. **It is important that there is collaboration and cooperation between and among all stakeholders** and herein lies the strength of scrum; everyone working together for a common goal. The sprint review is one event that allows stakeholders a formal opportunity to feedback.

Scrum Specific Principles

1. Scrum's **Empirical Process Control** principle highlights the main philosophy of Scrum, which is based on the three main ideas, which are transparency, inspection, and adaptation, which I explained earlier.

2. The **Self-organization** principle focuses on the modern workers, who bring in considerably superior value when self-organized. This quality results in better team buy-in and shared ownership of the project; and an inventive and imaginative environment, which is more favorable for growth.

3. The principle of **Collaboration** centers around understanding that each member of the scrum team is adding value from their own perspective. Once this is understood, the team can respect each person's role, listen to their point of view and use these perspectives to build a higher value product. Each member must ask themselves, how can I work with my peer for the good of the product.

4. **Value Based Prioritization** is a principle that emphasizes the focus of Scrum to focus on features that provide the maximum business value starting from the beginning of the project and going on until the end. The product owner combines this with the 80/20 principle to get early return on investment.

5. **Time-boxing** explains how time is regarded as restrictive in Scrum. Time boxing is usually to help manage product both project planning and its implementation effectively. Time-boxed components in Scrum usually include Sprint Review Meetings, daily scrum meetings, Sprint Planning Meetings and Sprints.

Now that you have a strong foundation in agile scrum and since this class is centered on the scrum product owner, let's put our focus on this role as we move forward.

Agile Product Owner: A Deep Understanding

What Is A Product Owner?

The product owner stands in as the representative of the business and its customers and therefore considers the stakeholders' interests on behalf of the company. His/her responsibilities partly involve having a vision of what he or she intends to develop and then conveys that vision to the development team. This is central to effectively and efficiently commencing any scrum project. He or she is responsible for warranting the value of work the team produces.

The product owner is commonly a lead user of the system itself, or someone from marketing, product management or anyone with a concrete understanding of the product's users, the competition and the projected tendencies of the product being developed. This enables him/her to have a crystal clear vision of what they are to build. He/ she is in charge of the intensification of business value, i.e. ensuring that there are returns on investment. He or she defines and owns the vision of the product in addition to owning the product backlog (the list of features to be developed). To give you a better understanding of all this, let's take a closer look at some of the roles that the product owner undertakes:

- ✓ Identification and prioritization of the product features (also called stories)

- ✓ Creation of acceptance criteria for product features

- ✓ Decides the right shipping times of the functionalities

- ✓ Decides whether or not development should carry on, on a given feature

- ✓ Accepts and rejects the presented product increments

- ✓ The final arbitration of requirements and questions about the project rests upon him/her

The product owner does not have to be physically present in all meetings but has to be reachable to respond to questions. He or she will also contribute as a scrum team member.

Among the product owner's key skills should be communication. The product owner is the mediator between all the people involved and interested in the product and s/he has to be the one who knows what to say, when to say it and to whom to say it. Basically, s/he has to be able to communicate appropriately with the stakeholders, users and development team among others.

Traditional Product Development vs Scrum Product Development

As indicated in the beginning of the guide, agile was started to correct the traditional methods of software development, like Waterfall. Let us therefore go on to see what is so different between the two in terms of product development.

The **waterfall model** is a process, which follows a sequence. The development stages progress consecutively and the model is seen as flowing fairly smoothly downwards, the way waterfalls do. It follows particular phases in the development process and these are analysis, followed by design, then implementation followed by testing and finally maintenance. For the work to proceed to the next phase, the preceding phase has to be completed.

- Waterfall places overall responsibility on the project manager who should plan for the work.

- It operates on the 100% - 100% rule implying that you get 100 % results from 100% work input.

- There are no plans to modify the initial plan in place and developers should try not to. It even has a change control board in place, for any changes, which have be made.

- Product development is ordered depending on what the involved technicians want and not by discussion as the system assumes that all that should be known about the development is known upfront and so does not provide for 'during the process learning'.

- Waterfall does not provide for the development of features in early stages of development. Any working software will only be realized very late in the development process.

- In Waterfall, the developers do no planning but merely execute the work given for them to.

- Waterfall promotes analysis paralysis because the system does not provide for early testing of product.

The differences in the two are so glaringly clear. It has to be clear that the problems in the waterfall model are not any error on anyone's part. When software development started way back then, this was the available production method and was very apt for producing goods at that time. Due to the desire for earlier delivery with higher quality and value, realized that there were more beneficial methods.

How Is The Product Owner Different From A Traditional Product Manager?

There are many similarities between the traditional product manager and the scrum product owner, which include responsibilities like understanding the market, explaining the functionality of the product, and preparing the product launch among others. These similarities in roles make the traditional product managers the right candidates for product ownership but there is more to product ownership than the traditional roles undertaken by the managers.

A product owner has a more challenging task as it involves much more including but not limited to strategic duties like envisioning the product and managing the product roadmap in addition to the more tactical ones of collaborating with the scrum team throughout the development process, release planning and managing the stakeholders. The traditional product manager's role is more of a command and control one as opposed to the product owner's, which is collaborative and facilitative.

Where the traditional product manager's role was mainly a one man/woman job, the product ownership job is more collaborative i.e. product owner, scrum master and development team.

A Day In The Life Of A Product Owner (Including Typical Stakeholders)

1. Attend daily stand-up meeting with Scrum Master (SM) and Development Team (DT) to understand yesterday's progress, today's goals and how to overcome any expected impediments

2. Have a chat with some developers to get them clear on the project features they are working on

3. Have a discussion with SM about an impediment the visual designers encountered and details of how it was solved.

4. Start prioritizing backlog items depending on the value they bring to the company

5. Meet with stakeholders to discuss the budget for a future product release

6. Meet over lunch with one of the business owners and discuss the status of a new product release

7. Together with the SM, attend release performance testing meeting and discuss how best to include distant stakeholders in retrospective reviews.

8. Have a voice call with a stakeholder who could not make it for the finance meeting

9. Meet with SM to go over the findings from retrospective.

10. Attend sprint review on progress made with product during this sprint.

The list is by no means exhaustive but is only a general overview of how challenging the work of a product owner really is.

To assist in the daily duties, product owners can make use of road mapping to show the direction the product development is planned to take.

What Is A Product Roadmap?

A product roadmap is a high-level plan that explains and demonstrates how the product is expected to develop. It is built by product owners and should take market trajectories, value proposals and engineering limitations into account. It typically shows the incremental nature of how a product will be developed and delivered over a period of time and also indicates the important factors that drive the individual releases.

	1st quarter	2nd quarter	3rd quarter	4th quarter
Date				
Name	version 1	version 2	version 3	version 4
Goal	Acquisition: Free app, limited in-app purchases	Activation: Focus on in-app purchases	Retention	Acquisition: New segment
Features	• Basic game functionality • Multiplayer • FB integration	• Purchase dance moves • Create new dances	• New characters and floors • Enhanced visual design	• Street dance elements • Dance competition
Metrics	Downloads: top 10 dance app	Activations, downloads	Daily active players, session length	Downloads

What would a produ MDM road map look like?

Skeleton roadmap from http://www.romanpichler.com/blog/agile-product-roadmap/

The roadmap enables the stakeholders to express where they want the product to go, and why the product should be considered a worthwhile investment. The product roadmap also fosters learning, developing and requests for change from stakeholders. Having a goal directed roadmap is a great way to achieve the afore-mentioned. In contrast to a roadmap dominated by too many features, a goal oriented roadmap is based on goals.

Although there will be some differences depending on the product being worked on, a typical roadmap will state all the important dates when significant indicators are to be expected, the name of the product being developed, the goal of the product, it's key features and functions, and the various metrics for every significant/major product version or release. One good thing about a goal oriented roadmap is that it usually shifts the entire conversation to discussing agreed shared goals instead of arguing over different product features. This allows agile teams to have high level goals while focusing on the finer details in their sprints.

How Does A Product Roadmap Help You Build Products?

Because work on the product starts as soon as an idea is formulated, the roadmap can therefore be utilized to visualize the idea and make it into a concrete vision. The power of the roadmap lies in that it starts building the product before it is put to use, i.e. while it is being built. As the product owner and the developers work on logistics of the roadmap, many of the strategies which will be useful for the project come to the core and these will assist in making the development of the product as much of a breeze as can be expected in agile. It acts as a forecast of sorts.

Once a roadmap is built, it needs to be shared with the entire product team to ensure that everyone understands the vision behind the product and direction to be taken. Product owners typically create their roadmaps in PowerPoint and spreadsheets, and then email the slides and spreadsheets out to the team but it is becoming trendier to just post it online (using different collaboration tools like Google Docs, Dropbox, Evernote and other tools) to ensure that everything is available at the touch of a button. Reviews and updates are easier to post and conduct and get to all stakeholders that way. Responses are also immediate.

In the same way a road/route map directs the road user to get where s/he want to go, the agile roadmap smoothens everything on the product development route to successfully arrive at the final product presentation. The following points indicate how the roadmap does that.

✓ It ensures alignment between corporate objectives and product deliverables without which it might be difficult or virtually impossible to get a budget set aside.

✓ It makes it easy to identify product requirements to counteract impediments.

✓ It helps determine high-level time frames.

✓ It helps set and try to maintain the pace.

✓ The team can easily make adjustments on the fly as product priorities change.

✓ It enables easy collaboration because it is easy to keep everyone updated of progress or lack thereof.

✓ It makes it easier to visualize and communicate product strategies.

✓ It helps categorize requirements and effectively prioritize them for the betterment of the product

✓ It helps teams to know what their current commitments are and what the plan of action entails and aligns all stakeholders to current position.

✓ It creates a broader contextual awareness of workload, which helps the development team keep things in perspective.

✓ Feedback is immediate and this makes is easier for it to be integrated into planning circle.

✓ It enables the team to execute the plan of action as expected and as a result give them a sense of personal satisfaction, which is crucial for development of product.

✓ The roadmap mentally and physically prepares the team for unforeseen impediments, which may arise as they work on product development

✓ It provides the context around the team's every-day work, and promptly informs any changes to prevent unnecessary delays.

✓ A roadmap responds to shifts in the competitive environment and allows stakeholders to swiftly put in counter-measures to cushion product development.

✓ It helps the PO to communicate how he or she sees the product development.

✓ For any product to win the company's support; it has to be aligned to the company strategy's strategies; the roadmap helps set the course straight.

✓ By predicting how the product is bound to grow, it is easy to show how the product helps your organization to reach its goals. As a result, this makes it easier to secure a budget for the product development.

✓ The stakeholders know every stage of the development process and can therefore coordinate and collaborate effectively in development activities.

✓ A product roadmap promotes effective portfolio management, as it helps harmonize the development efforts of different products.

✓ Using a roadmap supports and supplements the product backlog thereby enabling the backlog to focus on the tactical product development issues.

√ It maps outs the release schedule which can translate into individual release backlogs

√ It validates deductions about the product target group and the needs the product address.

Basically, the above points either directly or indirectly affect whether or not a product will be shipped mainly through ensuring that everyone in the company is on the same page throughout development of the product and make it a point that whatever impediments are faced, they are immediately known by all, and solutions are generated promptly to ensure plans made are implemented as swiftly as possible. This ensures no hiccups to development of a shippable product.

Key Principles To Use When Carrying Out The Role Of The Product Owner

The Product Owner should understand that he or she is fully responsible for ensuring that the final deliverables are met as per set standards and requirements. He or she is the only person who is responsible for managing the product backlog among many other things. S/he therefore has to:

- ✓ Clearly express product backlog items for easy understanding by all stakeholders

- ✓ Order the items in the product backlog to ensure achievement of best goals and missions

- ✓ Optimize the value of the work the Development Team performs because this is the basis of the quality of the final shipment

- ✓ Ensure that the Product Backlog is very visible, very transparent, and very clear to all, and shows what the Scrum Team will proceed to work on in the next step in accordance with the three core agile principles

- ✓ Make sure the Development Team clearly understands different items within the Product Backlog to the required level to ensure efficiency in execution of duties.

- ✓ The product owner can delegate appropriate duties to development team but accountability rests fully upon his/ her shoulders.

- ✓ His or her decisions should be fully backed up by the entire organization for his/ her work to be successful.

- ✓ The said decisions should be made visible in the content and ordering of the product backlog and needless to say, the product owner has to see to it that that is ensured.

- ✓ The development team can only work on the requirements as stipulated by the product manager for accountability purposes.

- ✓ Product owner has to ensure that active user participation is important and non-negotiable

- ✓ He or she has to empower the team to be effective and efficient decision makers in promotion of self-organization

- ✓ He or she should bear it in mind that obligations for the product and conditions of development may change but the timescale is not flexible

- ✓ Should place focus on regular delivery of product

- ✓ Should ensure that each feature is completed before the team can move on to the next.

- ✓ The PO must ensure the 20/80 rule is applied throughout the process (as discussed earlier.)

- ✓ Should ensure that testing is incorporated all over the project development. There must be early and regular testing implemented. The earlier the user testing can commence, the sooner it can be incorporated into future sprints.

- ✓ It is important that there is collaboration and cooperation between and among all stakeholders

- ✓ The product manager should remember that she/he is a collaborator and facilitator but not commander or controller of the development process.

- ✓ Product owner should aim to produce maximum business value starting from the beginning of the project and going on until the end.

How To Create A Product Using The Scrum Framework

As discussed, product development progresses through a series of sprints (iterations). Sprints are time-boxed to between one and four weeks. It entails a number of different events (meetings). Here is a flavour of how you would be involved with each of these meetings as a product owner.

The (really) first meeting

This meeting is a behind the scenes meeting. It is the meeting during which the key stakeholders discuss their requirements for a product with the product owner. After a number of meetings like this, the product owner puts all requirements into perspective and aligns then with a vision for the product. In reality there may be a number of these meetings before the vision is finalised.

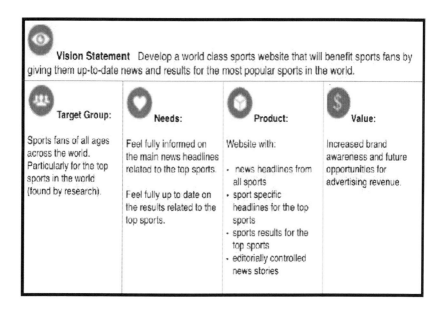

Vision Statement Develop a world class sports website that will benefit sports fans by giving them up-to-date news and results for the most popular sports in the world.

Target Group:	Needs:	Product:	Value:
Sports fans of all ages across the world. Particularly for the top sports in the world (found by research).	Feel fully informed on the main news headlines related to the top sports. Feel fully up to date on the results related to the top sports.	Website with: · news headlines from all sports · sport specific headlines for the top sports · sports results for the top sports · editorially controlled news stories	Increased brand awareness and future opportunities for advertising revenue.

This vision can later be used to form the roadmap.

The first team meeting

This is the product requirements update meeting. The product owner updates the scrum master and the development team of the requirements as stipulated by the stakeholders. S/he does this by presenting the product backlog (the list of features to be developed) which should show his/her vision in a simple but clear manner so that the others in the meeting fully understand his/ her position. The backlog should be presented in the form of from the highest priority to the lowest. This is usually a number of user stories on 3 by 5 index cards. The stories are called epics because they are large and unclear at first.

A partial sample of a sports website product backlog of Epics. Due to the large nature of the backlog, I have placed it on my blog with explanations. Just go to:

http://pashunconsulting.co.uk/blog/productbacklog.
html   *thats*
http://pashunconsulting.co.uk/blog/productbacklog.
html

Note: The User story title and acceptance criteria would usually be written on the front and back respectively of paper story cards. I have written them in columns to help visualize them in this class.

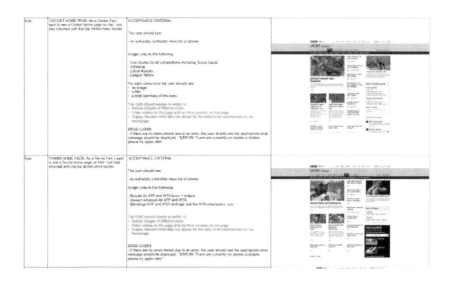

The product backlog grooming meeting(s)

Here the scrum team meet regularly to decompose the backlog into smaller user stories and estimate the backlog. This allows the team to familiarise themselves with the product and the product owner to get some early estimates. There are a few of these meetings before the backlog is in a state ready for a sprint. The backlog is estimated using a metric the team is familiar with. The popular method is story points (a measure of the size and effort of each user stories).

A partial sample of a sports website product backlog of estimated Epics. Due to the large nature of the backlog, I have placed it on my blog with explanations. Just go to:

http://pashunconsulting.co.uk/blog/productbacklog.html *thats*
http://pashunconsulting.co.uk/blog/productbacklog.html

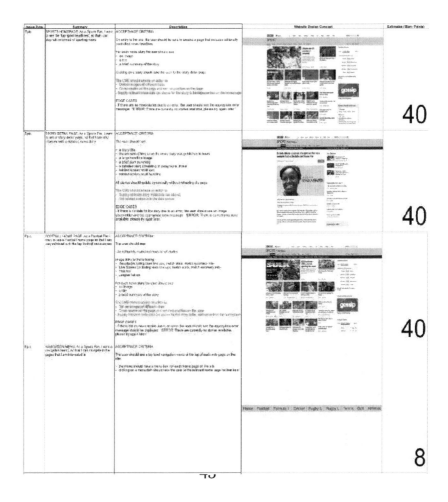

The sprint planning meeting

Once the team tell the product owner that they have more than enough stories to take on for a sprint, we are ready for our first sprint planning meeting. This is the first meeting of the sprint. This is also where the members of the team try to figure out the number of items they can commit to. In the same meeting, they create a sprint backlog, which is actually a list of the tasks they aim to perform during that sprint. The sprint planning meeting sets up the way forward for development of a product increment. It is in this meeting that they agree on the features to develop; ideally the one on the top most part of the product backlog.

One by one, the product owner talks through the top priority items in the backlog. The team breaks each item into tasks and accepts it into the sprint. This process continues until the team can no longer take on any more tasks (as all their capacity is used up.)

Note that the product owner gets no say about who does what as this is the choice of the team. Neither does s/he get a say in the number of items to be worked on in the sprint or choice thereof. This free reign gives the scrum team the desired self-organizing room.

By taking a minor set of product features from a given idea and developing them into a coded and tested functionality, they move a step towards achieving the ultimate goal because all the features developed in the sprints will, in the end, be integrated into the developing product or system; already coded and tested.

Daily scrum meeting

Every morning during the duration of the sprint, a stand up meeting should be held and attendance is compulsory for only the development team. I strongly recommend that the product owner attends this meeting each day to make immediate calls on anything holding up the team and to get a sense of progress. However a product owner needs to remain silent while the meeting is in progress. Any follow up can happen immediately after the meeting.

This meeting should not take a significant time to prevent eating into the production time; therefore, the meeting is time boxed to less than 15 minutes. In those 15 minutes, members of the development team share information about:

- the previous day's work

- the work they intend to cover on that day

- if there are any impediments to progress.

The scrum master usually facilitates this but does not need to be present. The team need to take the reigns of this.

The Scrum framework regards daily scrums as a way to harmonize and coordinate the team members' work as they talk about the progress of the sprint. The gathering also gives them a spirit of camaraderie and as they discuss individual contributions, they are empowered and better motivated to self-organize.

The sprint review meeting

At the very end of a particular sprint, the scrum team proceeds to perform a sprint review during which the entire team demonstrates how the product works. Any of the stakeholders who are involved in the project attend in order to give feedback with the potential to influence the next sprint.

- The feedback provided serves the purpose of making the final product better because, after feedback, the team might see it fit to make changes in the freshly delivered functionality to improve quality.

- It might also result in a change or addition to the product backlog, also potentially leading to improvement of final product.

- If a feature is approved in the review, it is said to be ready to be shipped i.e. to be used as part of the whole.

The sprint retrospective

The sprint retrospective is usually the very last thing that's done in a sprint and in most companies, it is done immediately after performing the sprint review.

Scrum stipulates that irrespective of how good a scrum team is, there will always be room for improvement. The purpose of the sprint retro is therefore to give the team members a chance to highlight the improvements, which they can do on the functionality. The meeting is attended by the product owner, the scrum master and the scrum team.

The retro normally uses three concepts:

- what worked

- what did not work

- what could be improved

What it means is that they (normally) brainstorm things they should start working on to improve the functionality, then they discuss those they should stop doing and lastly those they can continue doing, all in order to improve the product. Moreover, chances are that by the time the end user has the product, it is the best it can be.

Tips To Effectively Create A Product

To create a quality product, you have to remember at all times that you are working with a team. The three component roles of the scrum team should work well together to allow everyone involved to put as much effort as they can into the product and make one they will be proud of. You, as the product owner, have the reins to the product and you should, therefore; handle everything pertaining to the product in the best manner possible. The following tips and tricks will help you do just that. The only path to a good product is getting the best out of your team.

As you can note from what we've discussed so far, product development with scrum can be involving as a product owner. To make everything easier for you, here are some tips that will help improve your skills as an agile product owner.

1. Be as available as possible

Make yourself available for the team, but within reason. Even if you are not physically present, don't make reaching you be an impossible task. Being available allows the team to solve their issues early, which in turn allows them to maximize the chance of delivering on time to a high degree of quality.

I recommend giving them a variety of options for contacting you, such as

- face to face (preferred)

- telephone

- instant messaging (such as skype)

This will give you the best chance of success. Remember that nothing beats a face to face discussion or meeting. Therefore be sure to attend all the scrum meetings unless there is an emergency or urgent reason not to.

At the same time, be sure not to baby sit your team. Tactfulness is a necessity here, to give a healthy balance between availability and babysitting a development team. Help them help themselves and between you, you can have a great product.

2. Know your product

Inside out product knowledge is a big plus. Knowing your subject matter on the product in addition to the market will help you be better prepared to give updated feedback and guidance to a development team. There is no way you can try to build something that you do not know enough about, especially in a role where you have to let others in on your vision.

Do any background research needed for the product. This may involve:

- having good reasons in the product vision for the product's existence in the first place

- meeting with users to understand their needs

- keeping the last version of the product with you at all times

- meeting with other product owners to understand overlaps

- meeting with stakeholders to gather key information for user stories

Document your findings well and update the stories in the backlog with anything that impacts the team.

3. Be empowered without dictating

Being in charge of the product does not necessarily make you empowered, but for this role, you need to be empowered. Empowerment is psychological and an un-empowered someone cannot empower anyone. You therefore need to be empowered for you to empower your team enough to make them capable decision makers who are self-organizing.

Along with this, remember that you might be in the position of power as far as the product is concerned, but don't allow that to get to your head. You are in a leadership position but you are not a leader in the sense that you tell those in your team to do something and expect them to jump. If at all you have to, you suggest and give enough room for your suggestions to be accepted or rejected. You have your own areas where you can make exclusive decisions like in prioritizing stories and having the final say in what goes into the product.

When it comes to the duties of the development team, that is your no go area unless you are to work as a part of the team.

- You can collaborate with them on their duties

- you cannot tell them the stories they can achieve,

- neither can you tell them how much work they should select.

- It is especially not your duty to tell them they have to do more than their indications.

Unless there is need to doubt them (as in a history of incomplete stories), what they say they can do, take it that way; no more, no less. Motivate them, yes. Give clear guidance, yes. Assist if they ask, yes. Command them, no. You do not run the development team but you are part of the scrum team.

4. Practice humility

As product owner, you have the power to produce a good product in your hands. The major decisions lie with you but this should not make your head big. You deal with people knowledgeable in their areas and facilitating their work does not make you any better than they are. You need to ensure they are cooperative and collaborative and if you act superior, you will not have their cooperation and your team will not be collaborative.

Therefore I suggest you:

- think through suggestions from your team - especially product and feature suggestions as the team could be potential users

- understand when delivery is held up and do what you can to remove blockers (such as prioritising resources from the business side)

These two points alone will leave you streaks ahead of other product owners.

5. Be prepared

Preparedness is a requirement. There is nothing as easy as perceiving lack of preparation. The team needs to give you their trust and you earn it because the team knows that you are always prepared and responsible for the outcome of the product specifications and features. Do not drive your team to seek guidance from the next available reliable person, as this will be the result eventually. A few examples of tips are:

- always have the backlog easily reachable in terms of either paper cards or a tool that allows you to reach the stories easily. This will leave you prepared in any meeting or situation.

- bring blank paper cards to any meeting to capture requirements on the spot

- in the Sprint Review - again bring the backlog along and review the acceptance criteria of each story as the team are demoing the product to ensure that the features are 100% complete

6. Learn to communicate

If you are unfortunate enough not to be a natural communicator, for this role, you have to learn it. Practice it and fake it until you make it because the role just requires someone with more than average communication skills. You have to know how to effectively communicate in ways, which get your point across to all the different groups of people you will be dealing with throughout the process. Typical skills that make you are better communicator are

• listening to the other person's point of view, understanding and following up with your perspective

• negotiating an outcome with stakeholders by thinking of a win-win scenario

• displaying eye-contact and nodding your head to demonstrate understanding (even before you disagree)

These things will help you excel when working with teams and stakeholders.

7. Be reasonable but fun

This is a role that will benefit greatly from a positive character and humour. There are times when teams are against the wall and things are just not going the way they were expected to. Such is life and everyone will be tense but if the leader from a product perspective is tense, then this can worsen the situation. You can give life to your team and make the work worthwhile and your time together fun. Yes, it's work but it doesn't have to feel like it is all the time. Obviously we all want to create an atmosphere that drives teams to work hard and this can still be done by:

- being positive instead of aggressive whilst still reminding the team of the importance of the sprint and release goals.

- wearing a smile whilst still reminding the team of the impact on the business of missing the goals.

- providing rewards for timely high quality work such as away days or treats

- sharing jokes and humour with the team

The idea here is that by balancing a fun attitude to work with a focus on goals, you can help your team to succeed.

8. Know your role and those of the others

Knowing your role is the easy part as there are very few people who would get into such a challenging role blindly and without knowing what it entails; so, the assumption here is that you know your role. If you do not, act now! Read the scrum guide for starters. Not only should you know your own role, but also the roles of those you will be working with. Get to know what exactly is the role of the scrum master is, for example. As the product owner, you also have the scrum master's back, but that will be difficult to do if you do not know exactly what his or her portfolio entails. Moreover, it would not be possible for you to collaborate with someone whose duties are vague to you. You can surely help by re-enforcing the use of scrum rules and time boxes.

9. Instill Focus

Thoroughly explain it to your team that they have to be focused on what is on hand at all times during the sprint. Whatever product story is being dealt with at that time is the priority and all else on the backlog list should only be considered after the end of that current sprint. If your team multi-tasks to include features which were not decided upon in the sprint planning meeting, then the team will be losing focus and wasting unnecessary time and that can cost you a good product. Your team has to know what is at stake right from the word 'go'. Make sure your team understands that in the sprint planning and if you see the need, remind them as you proceed with development. The key times I suggest to re-enforce the sprint goal are:

- every day after the daily scrum

- at the beginning of the sprint planning meeting

- in conversations with individuals while working on requirements

Try to find non-repetitive ways to do this at the daily scrum. If the team seem to be on top of the goals anyway, maybe there is nothing to say. If they are going off on tangents, remind them of the goal straight after the meeting.

10. Stay on top of incomplete work

If at the end of the sprint there is any work undone or incomplete, then you have put it back in the product backlog and reprioritize it based on the current business value. If there are any doubts about the functionality, no matter how small they are, it means the product is not finished and in scrum accordance, that story heads straight back to the backlog. Stick to this; it works well for excellent products. If the same item is often incomplete:

- Understand what is holding the team back

- If it is a technical issue, ask them how they can solve it

- If it is unclear requirements, clarify the acceptance criteria

- Think about splitting the story into smaller separate stories

11. Practice the principle of less is more

Your team can only work on as much work as they feel they can do. You can't give the team more work than you feel they can complete; but giving them less is acceptable if you realize they might have got a little over ambitious. If, in the last sprint, your team had lots of work that's unfinished, try reducing the amount of work that you allocate to them in the sprint following. When agreeing to the stories your team can work on for the first time, limit the number of stories you bring to planning or can work on in the sprint. If they are really efficient and they run out of work before the end of the sprint, they can always ask you for more. The idea is not to hold them back from doing work, but to encourage them to ensure that everything they do is complete before going on to do more.

It may sound counterintuitive at first, but you will see that many problems come from teams biting off more than they can chew. This causes them to loose focus and in the end they get even less done than they would have if you gave them a smaller list of stories.

My advice is to ultimately to let them decide what they can take on (as they are the development team after all), but if you can draw attention to a smaller feature set as your sprint goal, this will help them to focus. For example saying "This sprint I would be impressed if we could get the home page and sports home page done." focuses the team more than "This sprint I would be impressed if we could get the all the home pages done."

12. Work closely with your team

This does not necessarily mean that you should be with them all the time, but be available for them as much as possible. Ensure you don't make your team members wait too long for an appointment since this not only wastes time, it also demotivates them. Plan to avail yourself unless you are really tied up somewhere like in a meeting with the stakeholders etc. Even then, try to keep your diary free to cater for the period right after any Daily Scrum as well as the Sprint Planning meeting. These are mostly the times when issues are raised up and being there to answer questions will keep the work flowing smoothly. Remember that you should not let your team climb walls to get to you but at the same time don't make babies out of them. Keep that balance and things should work out just fine. I suggest you:

- Be a team player. The team is the controlling mechanism in which the product will eventually be built

- Collaborate with the team in regards to giving them enough info promptly.

- For difficult team members, use a healthy balance of understanding their perspective and asserting your right as a product owner when it comes to requirements.

- Take care to act within your role and let them perform theirs.

- Be on hand to explain and discuss requirements (usually in the form of user stories) to any development team member whenever possible.

These tips will help them to deliver to your requirements. It helps them to help you.

13. Make your priorities strict

As the product owner, you have the vision for the product and you know the most essential components of your product. Therefore, when you come up with your product backlog, make sure those items are on the top of the backlog. You really have to know how to prioritize for this one to work well. Start with stuff that your users are likely to use every single day, which in most cases makes it the most important. Work on those features, which make the product a product, before you go on to work on things which make it better. It is very critical that you focus only on the essentials first then you can incorporate flexibility and luxury later on. The 80/20 rule tells us that focus on the top priorities will pay off! To do this I suggest:

- give each story a business value rating based on metrics such as user likeability, revenue, number of requests or similar. It can be a number in the 1-100 range for example

- prioritize high rated stories to the top of the backlog

- ensure that work on items lower down the backlog only occurs if there is no way that items higher up can be started

14. Do not include un-necessary features

You are in charge of developing a product that will be used by millions all over the world. Ensure that the product features you develop are going to be used by the majority of the users most of the time. Do not think that just because you can do it, then you should do it. Only after careful deduction can you decide to include features so, if you really analyze it and doubt the usefulness, then stop creating it. Never develop features no one is going to use. By getting rid of them, you can be sure you will improve productivity enormously. The company has trusted you with that power but doing anything out of bounds is abusing the power given to you. I suggest you:

- relate every feature in the product to some user research

- don't be afraid to remove features from the backlog even after a sprint review if you later find out that they are useless or business value has changed

15. Encourage your team to finish what they start

There are times when we bite more than we can chew. That is expected here and there. However, this should not be the norm. The same applies to your team. Let them know that if at all they start something within the sprint, they should strive to finish it. If your team leaves too much work unfinished at the very end of a sprint, try asking them to find ways in which they can leave less work undone at the end of the sprint. Just ask them kindly and they won't feel as if you are pushing them too far. Instead, help them find ways, like merely asking them to handle less. Remember that unfinished work (as opposed to un-started is eating into production time and wastes resources. Insist on them finishing what they start! If there are re-occurring technical issues, work with the scrum master and lean on him to coach the team on how to overcome these as quickly as possible. Remember that one of the scrum master's key purposes is to help you and the team overcome impediments.

16. If your team asks, assist them

Have you ever heard of servant leadership? This is something that the scrum master is charged with providing, but it is something we all can apply to our advantage. If your development team asks for help while implementing ideas if you truly can make it happen, and it has the potential of making the product better, do it for them. They are mature professional people and they will not usually ask for something for the sake of asking. Avoid having the misconception that you are doing too much for them already; collaborate with and help them as much as you can. They come to you because they believe you are the one to make it happen. Typical examples of this are:

- Leveraging human resources from another team (via your product owner colleague)

- Obtaining devices or software with business budget

- Giving advice on a technical solution from a user's perspective

-

17. Respect your team's space

The scrum model gives each one in the product team enough room to work to their maximum potential. You, the scrum master and the Development Team, all have your spaces. You are their product owner but you have to trust them enough to let them do what they know best. Do not step on their toes because this might make them think you do not believe in their abilities. Working together and collaborating will enable you to develop patterns that work well for you as a team and for the individual roles; respect those and the team will respect your station too. Be sensitive to their actions so that it will be easy for you to know when they think you are over-stepping your boundaries because sometimes you might do it out of habit but without having any ill intentions.

18. Make sure user stories are clear and concise

Write your stories so that they are easy to understand. Keep them brief and to the point. Avoid terms, which would be confusing and especially avoid ambiguous terms. Write your stories in active voice. Be sure that you only concentrate on the important details, and leave out non-essential material. You can use the popular Rachel Davies' story template to give you guidance. This template puts the user into the story and makes the story's benefit very clear.

As a <user role>, I want <requirement> so that <reasons/return on investment>

e.g.

As the game player,

I want clear and easy to follow instructions,

so that I do not spend too much time trying to figure out how to play the game.

19. Show your scrum master you value him/ her

Your goals for the team and the scrum master's roles are intertwined. Your scrum master's important role is to help the team and ensure that they get better at doing what you, the product owner needs them to do. Work harmoniously and collaboratively with your scrum master. Show him/ her everything about the project his/ her position justifies that s/he knows and the benefit to your team, and indirectly to you, will be immense. A good scrum master, once s/he realizes that you are collaborative enough, will assist you to balance your role and the team's work in a way you would find it tough and in some cases even impossible, to achieve on your own. You might be a master of your product and all that you envision it to be. He or she knows a lot about scrum and he or she will use this information to benefit your team and ensure it performs up to scrum standards, if you show that you appreciate the work s/he does.

20.   Make responsible decisions

As the product owner, you have the subject matter expertise and the vision of the product and resultantly you, are expected to make vital decisions about the product. Some of the decisions you will find yourself making, from time to time include, but are not limited to;

- whether or not a particular feature is necessary

- whether it is top priority and should therefore be released in the earliest days of development etc.

Your role defines that you can prioritize and/ or reprioritize the requirements of the product; and of the product features, as much as you see fit as the team moves through the development process. You work with the development team to consider the pros and cons of what needs to be done and eventually your decision should be one that benefits the business. You also assist the development team in making critical decisions about the definition of 'done', on the nature of testing which may be required, and the meticulousness, which your team might have to apply when testing for some vital functionalities. Bear it in mind that arriving at the correct user stories and acceptance criteria is a collaborative effort between you and your team. However you have the final say as what goes into the backlog and you should be able to explain your decisions at all times.

Take your role seriously enough and do all that is expected of you in the manner that you should. You are supposed to be the ambassador of product and if you lose track of progress, then you can be sure the entire process goes to waste. The development team may be empowered and self-organizing but they need to know they can depend on you to do what you should. That is the only way you can make your product the way it should be made.

I also want to draw attention to maintaining the backlog and attending product backlog grooming meetings regularly. Updating the backlog based on stakeholder input and developments along with getting the team to estimate and discuss regularly will go a long way to being a responsible product owner!

21. Build good relationships with your stakeholders

Get to know your stakeholders' viewpoint while giving them yours. Be sure you understand their needs as much as you possibly can. One of the worst things you can do as a product owner is assuming what you think the stakeholders' perspective is, and making critical decisions based on that. Besides the obvious result that this will not endear you to them, this will be disastrous for the product you create. You may want to find out:

• What are their long term goals

• What are their revenue goals

• What does the perfect product look like to them

Along with this, try to meet in an informal atmosphere such as a cafeteria once in a while. This will help you build a relationship and create a relaxed environment. It will also make it easier to negotiate and get your point across.

All of this may seem minor, but it will make it easier to build a better product.

22. Manage unfinished user stories

Try as much as you possibly can to limit the amount of un-finished user stories in the backlog. Unfortunate as this is, if there are stories, which you do not finish in a particular sprint, manage them.

- Closely work with your team so that you can all understand the reason behind the failure to complete the story and the available ways to ensure there is no repeat performance.

- Re-evaluate the position it now has on the backlog.

- Have a discussion to decide the future of the user story.

- If it still has it, does it still add value to the overall product and is there any chance that it can still be a priority to work on?

- If you are in agreement that indeed it should remain a priority, work on the approaches to take; should you approach it differently this time or still do the same approach?

Discuss the outstanding work and find out how best the team can work on it (if that is the decision) to ensure it poses no more risks.

23. Use the tools at your disposal

Your product owner toolbox has many tools, which you can make use of to make your work easier. For instance, you can use:

- <u>burn down</u> **or burn up charts**, which show the amount of work remaining in a sprint or release

- **velocity tracking**; where the number of story points (or other metric) completed by the team is tracked for each sprint to show how they are building momentum,

- **story mapping**; where you engage your team in an engaging exercise of setting up the backlog on the wall

Don't forget that these tools make for excellent information storage aids and can help you in communicating at all levels, and with all concerned stakeholders within the team along with all outside stakeholders and the management.

24. Never sacrifice product quality for any reason

It is known that there are companies, which have minimal concerns about the quality of the product especially if they want it released on a particular date. If you are unfortunate enough to be working for such a company, they can ask you to increase your pace of product development to ensure the product is released early. This is a no, no. Unfortunately, you might not be in a position to tell them outright that your principles and work ethics do not allow you to do that as that might jeopardize your position. You do not have to tell them that and neither do you have to quit. Just ensure that when you start work on the product, your DoD (definition of done) is in place. A DoD is a list of tasks compiled by the team and this list stands for all the activities that must be done on the story before it goes into production. In your hands, this is a powerful weapon, which can say all the words that you can't say to management. Simply show them your DoD and explain that the product is not done until it meets these quality standards. Let them know the reasons for the items on the definition of done. It could include factors such as:

- Testing

- Design standards met

- Known Critical bugs fixed

If the company still wants to release the product, this is their concern, however at least you are able to give them the best possible reasons why the product is not ready. Also the development team should ensure that anything already complete adheres to the definition of done. Therefore you can always release what has already been built with confidence in quality.

25. Avoid role confusion

There are recorded instances of a new scrum master coming into the scrum team and for whatever reason; they do not get as active as they ought to right away. As a product owner, you know that there is no time to waste and instead of pushing the scrum master (which you shouldn't do), you take the bull by the horns and start to take care of the development team's needs the way the scrum master should, to the best of your ability. Once you do this, there is a mixture of roles that leads to sure confusion of roles. Moreover, you can be sure that once the scrum master gets his/her steam back, there is going to be mistrust between you and lots of conflicts. If the scrum master starts off weak, it is true that s/he leaves you no choice, especially if you are a seasoned product owner who knows the role of a scrum master well. The best way to avoid this is to:

- speak to the management to ensure that the company gets an effective and experienced scrum master.

Such a scrum master knows exactly what to do in any situation to prevent creating unnecessary conflicts.

26. Be clear about the handling of new input

Input can come in from different sources. It can come from the stakeholders, from yourself, or from your development team. It is okay (if not better) to accept the input whenever it comes but inform all those concerned that the input has to be placed on the 'unscheduled backlog' session of the product backlog. Be clear to everyone that before they add the input, they have to know exactly where to place it to prevent serious mix-ups. You, as the product owner, are the one with the sole responsibility to prioritize the input and place it on the rightful place on the product backlog. Do not be put under pressure by someone who comes to you saying he/she has important input to be handled. Be clear from the beginning that if any input is not placed in the right slot on the backlog, then it will receive no attention from you. Sometimes it pays to be firm and resolute.

27. Be sure of what to do in a meeting

Do not develop the habit of setting up meetings without clear guidelines of what to discuss or without making thorough planning for it first. Ensure that:

- you have an agenda in place and everyone knows the items beforehand so that by the time they make an appearance, they can relate to what will be discussed.

- you have to first identify the reasons you are calling for the meeting, and

- ask yourself what you think the meeting will achieve.

If there are other means of achieving the same objectives without the meeting taking place, ask yourself if it would not be better for the whole group and your production times if you used the alternative instead. Only if you are convinced the meeting is the best way, should you call for it. Remember, scrum is about removing impediments to create productivity.

As a product owner, you can achieve a more productive team by saving them time.

Conclusion

We have now come to the end of this class; I am positive that it has taken you through your first stages of product ownership effectively as well as given you some tips for improving. You are well equipped to start the journey. With enough practice, and commitment, there is no doubt that you will go on to be an excellent product owner.

Thank you again for taking this class!

I hope this class was able to help you to improve and master agile scrum.

The next step is to start putting into practice what you have learned. All the greatest practitioners achieved their goals by putting tips such as these into practice and learning from their experiences. You can do it too!

Congratulations
HAVE FUN
WITH SCRUM
WWW.FREESCRUMEBOOK.COM

Finally, if you enjoyed this class, would you be kind enough to leave a review?

Thank you and good luck!

Resources

https://www.mountaingoatsoftware.com/agile/scrum/product-owner

www.innolution.com/val/detail/product-owner-day-in-the-life

https://www.linkedin.com/pulse/day-life-product-owner-scott-gibson

https://msdn.microsoft.com/en-us/library/hh765980%20(v=vs.120).aspx

http://www.romanpichler.com/blog/new-product-development-with-lean-startup-and-scrum/

www.romanpichler.com/blog/the-product-vision-board/

https://www.scrumalliance.org/community/articles/2009/january/the-product-vision

https://dzone.com/articles/working-product-vision-board

www.romanpichler.com/blog/working-with-the-agile-product-vision-board/

https://www.mountaingoatsoftware.com/agile/scrum

https://www.scrumalliance.org/why-scrum

http://www.scrumhub.com/what-does-a-scrum-master-do-all-day/

https://www.mountaingoatsoftware.com/agile/scrum/product-backlog

www.allaboutagile.com/how-to-implement-scrum-in-10-easy-steps-step-1-get-your-backlog-in-order/

www.scrum-institute.org/The_Scrum_Product_Backlog.php

https://www.mountaingoatsoftware.com/agile/user-stories

https://www.cprime.com/resources/what-is-agile-what-is-scrum/

www.agilenutshell.com/

https://www.mountaingoatsoftware.com/blog/make-the-product-backlog-deep

https://www.mountaingoatsoftware.com/agile/scrum/release-burndown

www.enfocussolutions.com/the-three-c-s-of-user-stories/

https://www.mountaingoatsoftware.com/agile/scrum/task-boards

http://www.scrumcrazy.com/How+I+Classify+Coaching+Advice

Preview Of 'The Scrum Master Mega Pack'

This book is an amalgamation of the following books sold as a cost effective box set (so be sure not to buy them again):

1. Complete Overview of Scrum - The Power of Scrum, In the Real World, For the Agile Scrum Master, Product Owner, Stakeholder and Development Team

2. 72 Reasons Why Scrum Works, For the Agile Scrum Master, Product Owner, Stakeholder and Development Team 3. The Scrum Checklist, For the Agile Scrum Master, Product Owner, Stakeholder and Development Team 4. Scrum of Scrums, Agile Programme Management, For the Agile Scrum Master, Product Owner, Stakeholder and Development Team 5. Scrum Top Tips, For the Agile Scrum Master, Product Owner, Stakeholder and Development Team

6. How to Become a Scrum Master, In 7 Simple Steps, For the Agile Scrum Master, Product Owner, Stakeholder and Development Team

7. How to Meet a Project Deadline with Scrum, In 7 simple steps For the Business, Agile Project Manager, Scrum Master, Product Owner, and Development Team

BONUS

8. Kanban, The Kanban guide, For the Business, Agile Project Manager, Scrum Master, Product Owner and Development Support Team

Here is a piece from the book:

6 reasons why SPRINT PLANNING works

Background

The sprint planning session is a meeting in which the team plan and commit to the stories that they will work on in a sprint. The meeting lasts no more than four hours for a two-week sprint. There are two halves to the meeting, the "what" and the "how". In the first half of the meeting, the product owner presents the list of features that he would like the team to deliver from the product backlog. He explains them and the team ask questions. In the second half of the meeting, the team breaks the stories into technical tasks and estimate them. The meeting ends with a commitment from the team to complete the sprint backlog within the sprint.

Reasons

1. The planning process gives solid understanding: As opposed to other methods, it is the act of discussing and understanding the proposed sprint backlog that gives the team a solid understanding of what they are building. There is no reliance on a document to do this.

2. Expert estimates: The estimates given at planning are from the most reliable source possible – those doing the work, as opposed to a single team lead.

3. Reliable estimates: Rather than individual estimates, the shared view of the team is reflected in the estimates. This is a more reliable view since it takes into account all perspectives.

4. Motivating, enjoyable experience: Planning gives a chance for people to interact and to some extent socialize. This is usually seen as an enjoyable experience as long as it is strictly timed and especially if planning poker is used as a technique (doughnuts also help greatly).

5. Product closer to customer desires: The product owner brings the business view to the session and the team brings the "builder's" view. This results in a product much closer to what the customer desires.

6. Strict time-box keeps morale high: The time-boxed session must run to a strict time scale. A further session can be planned if absolutely necessary, but this strictness prevents fatigue.

To check out the rest of (Scrum Master Mega Pack) on Amazon go to: http://www.amazon.com/dp/B00988FMU8

Check Out My Other Books

Below you'll find some of my other popular books that are popular on Amazon and Kindle as well. Simply click on the links below to check them out. Alternatively, you can visit my author page on Amazon to see other work done by me.

The Power of Scrum, In the Real World, For the Agile Scrum Master, Product Owner

Confessions of a Scrum Master, for the Agile Scrum Master, Product Owner, Stakeholder and Development Team (Inspired...Aug 12, 2014

Kanban, The Kanban guide, For the Business, Agile Project Manager, Scrum Master, Product Owner and Development...Aug 12, 2014

How to Become a Scrum Master in 7 Simple Steps (Agile Project Management)Aug 12, 2014

Scrum of Scrums, Agile Program Management, For the Agile Scrum Master, Product Owner, Stakeholder and Development...Aug 12, 2014

Scrum, The Complete Overview and Guide (Boxset), For the Agile Scrum Master, Product Owner, Stakeholder and Development...Aug 12, 2014

The Scrum Checklist, For the Agile Scrum Master, Product Owner, Stakeholder and Development Team Aug 12, 2014

How to Meet a Project Deadline with Scrum In 7 simple steps For the Business, Agile Project Manager, Scrum Master...Aug 12, 2014

Scrum Top Tips, For the Agile Scrum Master, Product Owner, Stakeholder and Development Team Aug 12, 2014

Selling Scrum to the Business: 72 Reasons Why Scrum Works, For the Agile Scrum Master, Product Owner, Stakeholder...Aug 12, 2014

Scrum, (Mega Pack), For the Agile Scrum Master, Product Owner, Stakeholder and Development Team Mar 28, 2013

If the links do not work, for whatever reason, you can simply search for these titles on the Amazon website to find them.

Bonus: Subscribe to Download the FreeScrumEbook and Bonuses

When you download the FreeScrumEbook and subscribe to get the free bonuses via email, you will get free access to a some of exclusive subscriber-only resources. All you have to do is enter your email address to the right to get instant access.

These exclusive bonuses and resources will help you get more out of agile scrum – to be able to reach your agile scrum goals quicker and faster than ever before like the pros. I'm always adding new bonuses and discounts as well, which you will be notified of as a subscriber. **These will help you to achieve your goals as quickly as possible!**

Here Are The Details Of What You'll Learn:

The Number one Reason why projects succeed or fail, which is key to your success going forward.

How Agile relates to Scrum one of the most confused topics in industry

A complete introduction to Scrum theory, the foundation of its success as the theory will give you a strong foundation going forward

An overview of all the Scrum rules so that you can set the correct framework for your projects

A complete understanding of all the Scrum roles as these make scrum so powerful

An overview of all the Scrum events so that you have a summary of all the practices the pros use

How you can take steps to get your project to the next level so you know what to do next

Access to my blog including:

Regular lessons on how to improve scrum events

Discounts of up to 99% on all my scrum courses

To get instant access to this free scrum ebook and more incredible bonuses and resources, click the link below:

FreeScrumEbook and Bonuses can be accessed here: http://www.freescrumebook.com

62508244R00056

Made in the USA
Lexington, KY
09 April 2017